nowhere
but
light

nowhere but light

Ben Belitt   Poems   1964-1969

The University of Chicago Press · Chicago and London

Acknowledgment

Certain of these poems have appeared in *The Virginia Quarterly Review*, *The Bennington Review*, *Voyages*, *The Nation*, *The Southern Review*, *The Quarterly Review of Literature*, *Mundus Artium*, *Encounter* (London), and *Poetry*; "Late Dandelions," "On Quaking Bog," "View From the Gorge," "Winter Pond: Lake Paran," and "Papermill Graveyard" appeared in *The New Yorker*. I am grateful to all for permission to assemble them in this volume. Section One of "The Gorge" and the first three sections of "The Orphaning," published as fragments of a work-in-progress in my previous volume *The Enemy Joy*, now may be read here in their completed form.

B.B.

Standard Book Number: 226—04194—8 *(clothbound)*
226—04195—6 *(paperbound)*
Library of Congress Catalog Card Number: 70–108879

The University of Chicago Press, Chicago 60637
The University of Chicago Press, Ltd., London

For Bobbye and Gittel

"*There is nowhere but light.*"

Contents

I

The Antipodal Man

The Orange Tree

To be
intact and unseen,
like the orange's scent
in the orange tree:

a pod of aroma
on the orange's ogive of green
or a phosphorus voice
in the storm of the forge and the hammer:

to climb up a ladder of leaven
and salt, and work in the lump
of the mass, upward and down
in the volatile oils of a wilderness heaven:

to sleep, like the karat,
in the void of the jeweler's glass,
yet strike with the weight of the diamond—
perhaps that is to live in the spirit.

So the orange tree
waits on its stump as the wood of its armature
multiplies: first, the branch, then the twig in the thicket
of leafage, then the sunburst of white in the leaves, the odor's epiphany.

All burns with a mineral
heat, all hones an invisible edge on the noonday, while the orange's scent
speaks from the tree in the tree to declare what the holocaust meant:
to be minimal,

minimal: to diminish excess, to pare it
as a child pares an orange, moving the knife through the peel
in a spiral's unbroken descent, till only the orange's sweat,
a bead of acidulous essence, divides the rind from the steel:

perhaps that is to live in the spirit.

Fat Tuesday

(Homage to Antonio Machado)

Yesterday's
seven-thirty still clots the band-stand
clock. A child sleeps near the tinsel and papier-maché
in a kerosene ring under the wavering flies.
The lovers embrace on the grand-stand

as slowly
the machinery of celebration engages
its spokes and wheels around the incandescent center
of their pleasure. The plazas sparkle like stages
with a blind bicarbonation, and the masquers enter.

How simply
their dangerous reversal
is accomplished, the permutations of concealment
turning the cheese-cloth and the mica of their disguises
into the dramatis personae of a dress rehearsal

and showing
the eye-hole's razor edges framing the double ovals
of the masquer's eyes, like buckets rearising in a well, glowing
with vagrant spontaneities, the amateur's surprises
caught in the act of his improvisations.

Knowing
those Tuesdays of the flesh, reptilian
in their hungers, Antonio Machado, dragging his horse-hair
great-coat, his *Irregular Verbs for French Beginners*, the chalky
bastinado of his calling,

through the parched
Castilian school-day, in ear-shot of a parish's explosion,
scribbled a maxim in his Marginalia:
"Not to put on one's mask, but to put off one's face: that
is Carnival; the face alone in the world—that is appalling!"

And watched
from a cindery tussock how the masquers circled
a fountain in Baeza, putting off his cheekbones, eyes, the sensuous
underlip, emptying his skull of what it held
under the make-believe regalia,

leaving only
the arm-band of the widower's long deprival,
the school-teacher who had "studied under Bédier and Bergson"
counting martlets between the bell-tower and horizon,
intent on the apocryphal and lonely.

And noted:
"The poet is a fisher in time: not of fish
in the sea, but the whole living catch: let us be clear about that!"
He put off his face, facing away from Madrid; the Tuesday of the guns grew fat;
he crossed the border into France, put on his mask, and died into his wish.

(*Antonio Machado [1875–1939], Spain's greatest master
of the "Generation of '89," lived out his life of widowhood
and deprival as teacher of French in the high school at
Baeza and died in exile in France toward the close of the
Spanish Civil War. Among his final works is a volume of
"apocryphal poems" and a celebrated collection of prose
"epigrams, maxims, memoranda, and memoirs" of an
"apocryphal professor" in whose guise he disclosed the
erotic and philosophical preoccupations of a lifetime.*)

Dog in the Manger

(For Daffodil)

Thunder has driven us
where darkness interprets the animal—
under the shears and the picture frames,
the gardening gear in the cellar—
to a furnace in banded asbestos
ticking its waterdrop sounds,
mop-cords of hardening naphtha,
pulverized ramshorn dung.

There, lives the crazed and unkillable
gift of her vigilance, the creaturely
fear that tightens the line of her jawbone,
while her fangs in their tortoise-shell
markings draw me into her skull
in a shine of bitumen
and we know ourselves frightened. We are stopped.
We look back toward the pillars

of garbage alive in the working aluminum,
storm-windows stacked, copper
and iron and oil, the gout of the gas
honing its tooth with a midsummer
midge's sound, to the troglodyte's world
that lies under the world of the human.
The house that she carries somewhere
on her back—a totem

of excrement, a shipwreck
of clapboards and shutters, an ark
that boils on the froth of the gutters—
rises and falls on its drains
while we watch for some presence
that troubled the waters. The darkness is heavy,
with a smell like a spade's wedge.
Our spittle is dry . . . We ride over the edges

together, and I call through the darkness:
Here, Daffy!
Here, Daffy!

Chipmunks

The sweet playfellow
is already aware:
taking a safecracker's stance
and turning the tumblers of air,
his paunch set down
like a reticule,
his ballerina's eyes
sootily bowed back
as for *Swan Lake*,
dancing the word for surprise
with his henna behind
and the tungsten crook
of his tail, his ears
like an adze
in the cinnamon and black
of his face's triangulations:

what draws love to its object,
unlike to like, impure to pure,
as my eyes to this?
The chipmunk, balancing the spike
of the acorn on prayed paws,
knowing the stations of the rodent,
finds kernel and meat
with his nose,
like any other rat,
and packs the pulp home
with his jaws;
by wainscotting and sewer
a killer keeps his vigil
by a trap:

Love is content with that.

Late Dandelions

The dandelions, wrecked on their stems
in a carnage of tentacles, conduits, and hoses,
clock-faces timed for a morning's explosion
that triggers the wire in the crabweed with its dynamite charges,
and detonates roses,

are a judgment. Crowding the clover and fern,
something demoniac, a gross Babylonian brass
hammered in sunburst and pentacle, Medusan or Coptic by turns,
a puffball of plumage on its way to a savage transfiguration,
is struck down in the grass

and time is made human again. O Angel
of process, who arranges the sequences
and interprets the seasons, how you wrestled
that night with the dandelion's changes, the wormwood
and work of mutation no watcher has followed,

the fiend in the bag of the mushroom, the corolla's
untimely unreason that forces its ores into feathers,
ravaged the tuft in the bubble, blew a planet away,
leaving only a space where seed after seed gathered,
and a scarab aloft on the stem revelation had hollowed.

On Quaking Bog

(For Jean Brockway)

When the walkers-on-water went under,
the bog-walkers came out of the barberry
thickets, booted in gum to their hips,
in a corona of midges, their ears electric
with sound, beating the stale of the swamp
with their whips and flailing the ground
for the itch under the frond, the fern's
demonology, the mosquito's decibel.

Night-sweat clotted their palms. They tasted
their gall. The sumac flickered a swatch
of its leaves in the lichens and venoms,
a dazzle was seen in the fog
as a vegetal world gave way to a uterine,
pitch pulled at their heels and blackened
their knuckles, the bog-laurel's fan
opened its uttermost decimal and showed them the Bog.

Paradisal, beyond purpose or menace, dewed
like the flesh of an apple with the damp
of creation, the disk of the pond glowed
under the dragonfly's bosses, where a faulting
of glaciers had left it—vaults of bog-rosemary,
buckbean and Labrador tea, a dapple
of leavening mosses soaking in ice-water, peat-wicks
feeding their gas to the cranberry braziers.

They entered the bonfire together. The moss
took their weight like a trampoline:
they walked on the sponge and bitumen without
leaving a footprint. In between,
in the vats of mat-roses where the waterline
closed like a skin, the ambiguous
world of imbalance, non-being, the pre-human
and tentative, was one with the ludicrous.

The quaking began: under their bootsoles
at first, like a whale under ambergris,
then cramming their wrists with a drummer's
vibrations, knocking their ribs and their knees
as all sagged and rebounded. They lurched on the wet
as though tracing a profile of breakers
or displacing the cords and the voids of a net,
and staggered back into their childhoods,

till their feet touched the granite again.
The Bog tossed them over the threshold
that opened a path in the spruce toward the opposite
edges. The leaves closed behind them. They walked
an unyielding and tangible world like strangers, remembering
only the hovering glare where the pitcher-plant's
hammer closed on the fly—the light shaking and shaking—
as a pulse touched their feet from below, and passed over.

Block Island Crossing

(For Mary Jo Shelly)

Crossing at Point Judith, one feels the world's
doubleness in the walloping stance of the ferry—
Elisha's marvelous flat-iron afloat in the fog
like a prophet's token: the boat and its baggage,
its plucky machinery, its cautionary noises,
swampy or soft-spoken, dividing the watery
flannels without wrinkle or seam, to its destination.

Below, inlanders, islanders. A stable
of station-wagons. The cold-drink and the hamburger
concession with its branding-iron's sizzle
of stabbed bicarbonation, tumblers of mustard,
under a gable of bulbs.
                        Outside, the yielding opalescence
and the steam, the nearly visible folding and unfolding
of the spaces, fog in its thermal channels
scudding the levels with a gull's evasions,
flying its semaphore of noises, bell-
clappers, conch-sounds, to a clutter of island pilings.

For, suddenly, it is *there*.

Somehow, in the drenched
displacement, a boat no bigger than a haddock
asserts its ungainly will to cross, with its gimcrack
universe intact, endures its self-effacement and its loss
and heaves a hawser to the opposite landing.

The Island
waits, placed and substantial. What was double or indistinct—
the rose-hip and the cranberry and the pure precipitation
that effaced them—merge in a common passion for existence.
Headlands and beaches, the Lighthouse in the middle
distance, open their burning vectors on the water
with a map-maker's precision, circle the air
with soundings to say where the rock was ambiguous,
the ferry's bow and the Village, a single vision.

There is light on the bluffs and light enough in the berry.
We know what the dove knows in our casual
chaos.

The gangway is down.

A mountain dries for us.

The Barrio

(For Felisa Calderón)

1. *The Well-Dwellers*

The hawk hangs in its fathoms
over the wild fig tree,
where Doña Porfiria sits in her clerestory of leaves
with an apron of shade and a pasta of wool
on her knees.

Turning the wool
on the square and her spindle of nails, she weaves
skin of the sky on the nude and carnivorous
colors from a ravel of threads on her lap.
A parakeet sharpens its quills on the tin of the cage.
The fig shows its flint
and the ripe avocado
packs its green marzipan under a nap of enamel.

The hawk looks the other way.
A thread in the skein
leads to the gravel-pits, the tar-paper splints
and the dove-cotes of Atzingo's well-dwellers,
the undesperate poor
whose courts are the floor of the mines—a ceramic
of pumice
when the Falls of Saint Anthony lowers its twine
in the drought; or floating its coops and geraniums in midsummer
mud that drops from a cut in the stone
and colors the rooftops with blood.

Doña Porfiria sleeps in a bomb-burst of figs
and ripe avocadoes. The ball on her knees
rolls away to the edge of a precipice
where the Barrio, caught
in its deathly siesta, immobile as bone,
glows on the web of the square.

There is red on the spikes
as the hawk strikes.

2. *The Corral*

The watered-satin
cummerbund of the placed young prince
in the corner of the picture, spread-
legged and slight
in an incongruous countershine of edges—

something out of Velásquez—
a light, maybe,
ashen and rose, that tempers a chalice's
outline, the withers and hocks of the horses,
where armies in an afterglow of straw
await a changing protocol of keys:

something equestrian, courtly, obsolete,
historical cruelty, the subservient upward look
from the stirrups
to the imperial rump in the pommels,
troubles this little corral.

A boy paces the three-year-old,
a cord's length from the nostrils' flaring transparency
veined like an orchid.
                    The animal droppings fall
smelling of iodine and seeds, the steam
of the horses' dung, medallions of goldleaf and flies:

as Mexico turns
with a papery sound of bougainvillaea,
flashing its doorways and distances—Velásquez's
carrousel—
contemptuous and civil,

and the young prince stares from his dream.

3. *Nativity*

Studying perfection, the charcoal-vendor's wife
scours down her barrack.
                              For the night of the Child
her table offers to all
the poor man's cornucopia: the syrinx
of the sugar-cane, slashed; cut-glass
of *Orange-Crush*; papayas laid open,
the anthracite of their seeds and the bonfire of crescents
together;
the shewbread, the crêche, and the knife;
the bed in the dark of the catacomb,
the crossbones and skulls of the peat.

Tonight, the dearth of the world
is immaculate. The cave and the stable
breathe on the birth of an animal,
make perfect their poverty, and the fullness of time
is complete.
Cut-paper mantillas, a tissue of festival lace
fly from the doorway.
                              The child in the bread
and the child in the broken piñata
sit down to their feast of desire and denial
while the candlewick lengthens like tinder.

Even the charcoal is beautiful. The sticks
drive their roots through the resins, pentecostal
and lost, the oils in the fern
open their scrolls, the bins of bitumen
send a column of myrrh in the soot.

And here is the child of the holocaust, bringing
a cut of the sugar-cane.

My hunger is great, and I eat.

4. *Salto de San Anton*
(Saint Anthony's Falls)

We are summoned, we know,
by no great thing—a sound's
excitement, the panache of the spray
on the quill of the waterfall—
to witness some self-expense:
a break in the river's bed
that opens the stone and makes it aerial.

We wait on the cavern's anvil,
not knowing yet
whether to complete or contain or demolish
the thing we would contemplate,
feeling addition and loss, the abyss's overplus,
the hammers of gossamer pounding the feathery glosses
while the stones take a thornier polish,

and the thing we would re-create, the withheld
and the given thing,
conclusive, apocalyptical—
the column of force aloft on the basin's edge
and the bow in the column—
fails in a sickle of water, a glow on the flat of a precipice
like light under a threshold
where the insomniac questioner turning the pages of water,
the troglodyte under the Gorge,
feels the bottomless cold of the source,
the burning away of the brim.

5. *Siesta: Mexico/Vermont*

The light that deals us less
and bears the eyelid down, like the pan of a scale,
to set our vision right—
predilections of ochre and pomegranate,
the cactus's belly-hairs, the jeweler's wedge
that widens the magnolia's claw—

delivers us blindfold to our upper and nether
senses. Searching transparency, we hear
the turning millstones at the center,
the infinitesimal pumice in the flaw,
curving the lenses, matching the incandescence
of the edges,

circling the precision
of a moment like a bareback rider's
hoop burning with spikes and gasses;
while the antipodal man
turns heavily in mid-air,
locking his flying foot-soles above and below,

enters the horizon's double ring, the tropic
and the polar fires—an icicle in Vermont
rayed like Guadalupe's mantle, the frost
on the machete's edge—head downward and head
upward, king of the playing-cards,
who sleeps in the slalom's angle with the Mexican.

The Termites: Taxco

This dust that wakens my dying
with the waste of the crossbeam—sawyer
of darkness that shows where corruption's
serration has worked in the wood

and passed through, leaving blight
on the pillow, tea lees, coffee grounds:
that lives in the knot and the grain
and rifles a roof-tree of light

with the smut of its daily cremations—
will not stay for an answer. Gomorrah
burns like a match-stick, and the mound of the termite
prepares its necropolis

in the cedar and teak of a table.
Under the rung of the chair
the axe falls, dead-center, the cone of the plummet
goes taut. A pylon of ash, like an

obelisk, widens on pumice. Murder
is worked in the wormwood
and cancer. Herculaneum's
twilight falls everywhere

while we wait for a plausible sound:
millstones; the tooth's edge on
the tooth; lava and mud. The palm
rattles its quill and the world

whirls once like a distaff
filling, bedded in linen and blood,
tensed to its slack. Light
smashes on cobble

for the vendors of sherbet and gelatin who keep
watch on a splinter of sack-cloth,
settle their sores and their stumps in Vesuvial
ash, wake once, and go back to their sleep.

II

The Gorge

"Out of this nettle, danger,
we pluck this flower, safety."

The Gorge

(Cuernavaca)

1. *The Gorge*

The jacaranda's color,
clocking the air like a pollen,
and the poinciana,
the palm's quill and the sprocket of flinty bananas,
come to me from a gorge's Gehenna. There,
in the kingdoms of ordure,
the bamboo's stave,
explosion of grasses where water is only a sound—
blood knocking a stethoscope, crepitations
that speak for the sybil from a navel of rubble—
the waste of a city works under mangroves
and is forced underground.
All that remains of the starved and appetitive
life, acid and gall, moves down
under feces and bandages, newsprint, a tin-can
necropolis, cat-gas
in the verminous cane, toward a darkness's
center where the rat mills its
plenitude.

I follow the gardens
aloft over gardens, the gush
of magenta, a shuttlecock seedling, toward
jacaranda again. *Yes: it is there, and it thrives,*
held by the eye to the cusps of those doubled
volcanoes, the male and the maiden; one, lying
drugged under snow, one erect
like a mace of magnolias,
while equilibrists toil on the slopes toward a purity,
soiling the sheaths for a toe-hold,
out of eye-shot, and the condor imagines perfection.

(Legend assumes that Popocatépetl and Ixtaccihuatl, one
vertical and the other recumbent, are male and female
principles, respectively. Both volcanoes are visible from
Cuernavaca.)

2. *View from the Gorge*

Doré knew this overhang—
he cut
his cortège for the damned, on those levels,
to carom on the magnets and springs, in the banging
of gongs and the lights of his pinball *commedia*.
In his black-and-white
world, the ascents and descents of the Gorge,
the roots like a fistful of entrails, the hachure
of pitchblende and acid that abuts
on that ordered logistics for sinners,
lead to a fall or a forge.
The odds
are already well-known: electric displays for the winners,
and the damned circling down toward the hammers.

What holds me today
is the purgatorial moment, seen small on the opposite side,
on the tilt of the slope where the gardeners
move in the marzipan whiteness squared off
like a waffle. Quicklime
has dazzled the glass of the greenhouses there,
sugared the ovens of Hansel and Gretel
where a work of redemption begins
in the alternate lines of the cuttings—bougainvillaea
and palm on the ledges—blazing giddily in buckets and tins.

Some loving solicitude has motioned the mannikins there
to hover like dragonflies and settle like seeds in the air—
to balance all day
on a long foot, for purchase, with the shorter
doubled into their shoulders—penitential, half mantis,
half angel, on a causeway of manna and boulders.

And the moment suffices.
What lies plane at the top
like a sponge-rubber glaze for an architect's table
or a primitive frieze for a ceiling,
what we guess from below, in the clot of the mangroves:
the generations of Rahab, the fires and the basalt of Dante, the bones
of the beast of Apocalypse, Quetzalcóatl
and Grendel in the offal and trash of our sins—
these were an earlier fable.
Inbetween, go the gardeners, with the grace of the hummingbird's
balance, who bend to the slope
in the quicklime and flowers, planting knowns
and unknowns, because sun shines exceedingly there
and the spirit is willing.

3. *The Loco-Bird*

The loco-bird flies over the Gorge,
tilts on a scrub-palm, at his metaphysical
angle, looks down from his glinting
propellers, and takes in his prize, at a glance.

                                                               All my need
for the marvelous, my awe
at the slant and equivocal—all
I have stood on its head in behalf of the wonder
that sharpens the bat's wit and tightens his decibels
to portents and sounds from down under,
is undone by his stance.
                            Whatever Zochipili heard
in the flint and the scoriae, the loco-bird sees
what is there to be seen:
two quicksilver drops on the cusp of a fern, and a turd.

Back in the tulipan, he rattles his beads
and enamels. Moving out of the down-drafts unawed
by obliquity, all's one to him: a
descent in a maelstrom or a herringbone
climb up a Matterhorn—the loco-bird swivels
his rudders, steadies his keel, and skates off,
chaplinesque,
on a rink, in the steerage, a spa, an alarm-clock,
a lady's emporium, a steam-bath with the peerage:
he knows how it feels
to look into the billy and badge of the actual
and veer out of range on his wheels
without ruffling his daily sensorium.

He fills the whole tree with his presence.
His tail-feathers take the expansive designs
that our grandmothers mounted in isinglass: India ink
on a background of spirals and pampas-grass, absurd in the litter
of florid calligraphy. He blackens the leaves
with the crow's iridescence,
while a sound issues forth from the glitter:
not madness, not the anger
of Timon, or Lear on the heath, but the gratified scream of the bird
of the abjectly ridiculous—a sound like a child's smutty fingertip
rubbing the damp of a shaving-glass; or a glass-cutter's wheel
over glass; whistles and burps; an acetylene blast;
and the banging of safe-cracker's tools in an empty museum.

All tumbles into the Gorge,
bounces off into nothing from level to level, is absorbed in the stream.
It says: *The devil walks to and fro in the world, the devil* . . .

But the bird in the tulipan tree has no answers.

4. *Flower Market*

The divers in Eden go down and return
from the well of the cobbles
with a festival target of flowers,
the roulette of the funeral wheel,
tinfoil, terracotta and fern,

in a bird-song of names: *El Clavel,*
La Orchidea, Rosalinda. Hands
work in the runnel of water, like fish,
looping wire in the floating corollas, unreeling
their roses like brackets of sponges, frames

for the wreath of the wicker,
dishes and jars where the honey-bee
strikes with a sound of exploding fuses,
and roots in a bandage of lilies.
A perishing

forest of stems, cut gardens
that fly under awnings and carrousels,
blacken in buckets. The clot
of the scathing carnation bores through a tunnel
of pollen, and falters. Midday

is limp on the stones. A reek, as of altars
and napkins, suppuration, the candlewick
flapping on wax, saints
in a strong-box of bones, charred
rocket sticks, gathers like marsh-gas.

Under a groundswell of plaster
the gutters slope toward a cut in the Gorge,
bleeding all color. Water-boys
wilt in the stalls. The shutter slams down
for the shopkeeper's lock. And night festers.

5. *"Gayosso" Ambulance Service: Emergency*
(Cuernavaca to Mexico City)

Feet-last,
on Gayosso's tea-caddy for corpses
and convalescents, all seemed an
"emergency." Already
the colors had charred in the tulip-trees,
batons and vibrations
barred on a cereal zodiac, while I rolled
underneath toward the van
in my onion of blankets.

The idea of non-being,
the broths and syringes, cocoons
of miraculous molds and detergents that spoke
of a "turn for the worse," swirled
in the headlights. The gorges turned backwards,
the city sloped under my shoulders in a rocket-burst
starring the Valley of Mexico. All tripped like a lens and a shutter
on the flare of a moment and spoke for the traveler:
                                        "Urgent!"

Urgent?
        And what of the fraud of that "safety?"
The clown climbing the clock in the celluloid,
the tortoise-shelled
stranger brilliant with nausea, caught
on the clock-face, on the pin and the pointer, riding
his belt-buckle, knows better . . .
                          One walks as one can
on the vertical
planes of the windows like ties on a trestle,
looking fifty flights down to a dumb-show of
Stock Exchange runners; one slips
toward the tooth of the buzz-saw
while the freight-cars bear downward from Toonerville,
sparkling with danger.

So the scene recomposes itself,
undemure in its aftermath, "drawn to scale."

Having rented a cut in the Gorge
in a weather where even the tiles on the facing embankment
are plain, one endures the precarious.
                              Always,
crossing the tulipans, somewhere,
Gayosso's "emergency" rides on the scream
of a moment: the lateral life of the "urgent"
centers and stays on an ego, like a carpenter's bubble;
the equilibrist falters,
shocked by his personal hazard.

                    But another sound
lives in the Gorge—
an equivocal thrashing of bamboo and manure and papyrus,
neither pure nor impure: the spirit
that works in the middle
stark under the sun-stone,
in the mash of the upper and nether.

                         And heard as the Gorge-Dweller
hears it, the serpent's tail beating the shell,
that unriddles its birth in the wet and the dark

And says: *it is well*. It is well.

III

The Great Cold

Cutting the Bittersweet

The quarrelers in bittersweet,
saviors and butchers, too late for stealth,
are here in the August morning, in the first of the heat,
with their stilted pruning-shears and their puritan hate

to root out the trespasser, berry and branch,
in a country vendetta. They have seen
how the strangler advances with trident and net,
forcing its pod in the thicket of lilac—

the gratuitous killer whose
grievance is everywhere, scribbling the margins
with threats, cutting anonymous letters
in the broadening leaf; who stabs through the stake and the splint

to gather a mangled typography
and extort the whole plenty of summer: the crime
that shows only the glint of its appetite, the red of the bittersweet
berry, to say what catastrophe means

and speak for the mindless destroyer. But justice
is manifest: a pruning-fork works
in the cluster, the noose of the bittersweet opens
in spirals and layers, disengaging

the rose and the poplar and surrenders its murderous
sign: a cutting of ovals and staves
like a musical signature, a bonfire alive on the stones.
And the searchers in bittersweet, those whom the summer

left nothing, the red-handed ones bereft in a winter
of holly—the parasitical borrowers,
time-servers, counterfeiters, the clingers and late-comers,
gather the harvest indoors.

Winter Pond: Lake Paran

(For Jo Van Fleet)

Lest the ripple deceive us
with its midsummer dazzle, a cat's-paw
of lustre on the shimmering weight of the water,
and the Heraclitean swimmer
dissolve into light, scarring the pond
with his passing—arm over arm in the herringbone ringed with a gas—
and no one believe us,

I stand in the March
of my mind in a winter perspective:
suds, scurf, cobble—a sherbet of blackening ice
with a pylon inset on a lunar enormity, and beyond
it a tractor in characterless orange;

the lake like an adamant
drawing into the flint and the salt
all a planet's mobility—algae and perch,
the gelatinous hives of the frog, night crawlers,
the semen and freeze of a winter—until
all locks like a cluster of crystal,
lifts up in its basin in its perfect containment,
a monolith crowding the shale,
a troglodyte's hammer
pounding the weathers and pressing on obdurate matter
like the light on the pomegranate's rind
or the bones on the scales of a carp.

The seasons disclaim us. But a shock lives on in the air—
a pulse, like a forge in a cloud
that beats on the latent and makes the ambiguous bearable.
Facet by facet, we assemble a vanished relation—
the swimmer under the ice and the skater on water—
harden the edge of our world till our images name us,
and the possible touches the heart and declares what it saw:
an ice-floe that burned in the thaw,
the hailstone's precipitation
that opened a well for the noon of the fish and the flycaster,
set a bow on the ripple, recovered the spinner's vibration,
till all was motion and passion and presence, flashing as never before,

and the swimmer arose in his nakedness and called from the opposite shore.

Cold

"The clock for the great cold stopped dead."—Léonie Adams

1

When cold froze the locks
and the alarm gave no sign of awakening,
I sank underneath, in the wheel-master's well of the clock,

and saw trapped there the great beast of Time
that eludes all the hunters,
pinned by a second on the claw of a ratchet, alive in its changes, beckoning.

the freeze at the heart of the world
unfolding the bone of the fiddlehead
icicle, cornucopias of maidenhair, asterisks of lichen and frost.

My breath stood forth on my face, Job's
spectre, sleeper in causes and compasses,
that hardens a block in the river

for the sailor's dead reckoning
—carborundum and mercury—
and writes in the book of the cold with iron pen and lead forever.

2

Cold moves in the legs of Socrates, soldier,
and music moves in the hemlock
of the flute-playing gymnast at his games in the mind

where death and its mourning apprentices, after the oracle's
horseplay, nude under glistening oils,
touch on the stones of the bath

with a satirist's laughter, and the sex
unsheathes on its stalk for the young man's dalliance
and the old man's tenderness:

discobolus: the intellectual cold
of the agora in a boy's Spencerian hand
writing circles and ciphers, push-pulls, staves of the musical line

in its freezing calligraphy, thought
working on thought
in a quicksilver column, while the ontological hero

toils on outrageous errands, the stables
are swept at last, and at the apple's end Hesperides
smokes in the rapist's hand: a zero on a zero on a zero.

3

In the house of the Snow Queen, I remember,
all smelled of acetylene. The strayed child
under the Turkish cupolas

drove the splintering flints of his gaze
over sand-castles and tundra,
his knuckles gouging his eye,

snowblind with loss and unable to cry:
while, for the sake of his grief,
cold turned to smoke on the nursery

window, unfolded enormous devices
of deprival and loss, the tree
neither evil nor good, and the cross in the garden of ices,

isometric, pubescent, joining the nipple and navel,
a rainbow boring the salt in a double relief—
an angle of onyx on a circus-rider's spangle,

ascending: a diamond on a diamond on a diamond.

4

Della Robbia's ceramic: this blue-and-white
hearth-bed of glazes holds no "loves" or madonnas,
plaques of ascending crevasses, reliefs to allure and invite

in a childhood's geography hardened to flour-paste
and traced with a map-maker's line. Nothing amazes.
The fiction of human direction

prints its necessitous footstep in the glare and the brine
and fails in a blind circumspection:
under the flake and the sparkle

a presence that grapples a continent, the glacier
that walks the moraine, the whole
heft of mica and gravel, alluvial conch and detritus

tilts halfway toward Asia, turns on its axle of coal,
dragging its fish-bones and flint-heads, iron and bronze in the ferns,
slips toward the pole

on a pendulum's back-swing. A heart-beat is heard in the rock:
and the cold, the great cold, the geysers of oracular cold
issue forth to the Pythoness.
                    And a ratchet resumes in the clock.

Papermill Graveyard

(North Bennington, Vt.)

In that country of thresholds we move like vandals,
overturning birth dates, death dates, necrologies, Bartlett's
Familiar Quotations, the exorbitant rhetoric
of compliment, spelling hard names, looking for pictures
under the blackboards of a child's stone library
of aphorisms. In the runt gardens and the greenhouse
"arrangements"—pinwheels of laurel in plastic, jelly jars
crammed with wildflowers not meant to outlast
an homage, the rancid memoranda of the very poor—
all is remembered. Each gives to each in the ghastly
plenty: the intimacy of a terminal cough
recalled in formaldehyde and licorice, a bull's-eye of death trance,
the husband's abandoned spasm in a barrow of granite,
endearments, betrayals. The tribal successions of the unexceptional man
are plausible here. Even the destitute scribble their heraldries.
The soldier schooled in a captive security, mistrusting the living,
salutes the interrogator with name, rank, and serial number.
Under the chintzy flags, holidays, holocausts, individual
deaths, the unlucky recruit, blinded by chevrons, is caught
in the scintillation of family keepsakes, a rabbit's foot
crossing the spaces in search of savory greens. All
remains minimal: footlockers of Government Issue
cut frugally to size, berry boxes for the stillborn,
mortuary cabinets indexed under Urgent Business
in an Erechtheum of furnished pillars
where death begets death and nothing comes of nothing.

Having nothing to memorize but an expatriate spirit,
her chemist-husband married, unmarried, remarried, the epithalamial
rasp of a cello string, and the kindness of friends who covered her loss
with a willow, I forage for trifles—the maggot's hammer-blow,
a lawnmower's blade in the chicory, my face on the bevel
of granite glazed over "Mother" and "Father."

But this is no trifle.

Jeanne Butler, Jeanne Butler, Jeanne Butler, how strangely you lean
toward the heel of my hand, still living on your nerves, severe in your Breton
cheekbones, repeating the uvular "r" for schoolgirls from Cambridge, settling
your napery while our teacups bitter in a garden
over pitted persimmons broken and eaten together, and a changing wind
works in the wafer's paste, hardens the knife's edge, and delivers
our unhaunted world to the Prince of Darkness!

Veteran's Hospital

(White River Junction, Vt.)

Bringing "only what is needed—essential
toilet articles" in a paper bag,
dressed as for dying, one sees the dying plainly.
These are the homecomings of Agamemnon,
the voyages to the underside of the web
that weaves and unweaves while the suitors gorge upon plenty
and the languishing sons at home unwish their warring
fathers, with strong electric fingers.
                              The fathers are failing.
In the Hospital Exchange, one sees the dying plainly:
color televisions, beach towels, automatic razors—
the hardware of the affluent society marked
down to cost, to match the negative afflatus
of the ailing, the bandages and badges of their status.
Under the sand-bags, rubber hoses, pipettes, bed-clamps,
tax-exempt, amenable as rabbits,
the unenlisted men are bleeding through their noses
in a perimeter of ramps and apparatus.

In that prosthetic world, the Solarium
lights a junkpile of used parts: the hip that caught
a ricochet of shrapnel; tatoos in curing meats;
scars like fizzled fuses; cancelled postage stamps;
automated claws in candy; the Laser's edge; and barium.
The nurses pass like mowers, dressing and
undressing in the razor-sharp incisions
and the flowering phosphorescence. The smell
of rubbing alcohol rises on desertions and deprivals
and divorces. It is incorruptible. A wheelchair aims
its hospital pajamas like a gun-emplacement.
The amputee is swinging in his aviary.
His fingers walk the bird-bars.
                              There is singing
from the Ward-Room—a buzzing of transistors
like blueflies in a urinal. War over war,
the expendables of Metz and Château-Thierry,
the guerillas of Bien-Hoa and Korea,
the draftees, the Reserves, the re-enlisters,
open a common wave-length. The catatonic
sons are revving up their combos in the era
of the angry adolescent: their cry is electronic.
Their thumbs are armed with picks. The acid-rock guitarist
in metals studs and chevrons, bombed with magnesium,
mourns like a country yokel, and the innocents
are slaughtered.

On the terrace, there are juices
and bananas. The convalescent listens to his
heart-beat. The chaplain and his non-combattive daughter
smile by the clubbed plants on the portico.

They shall overcome.

1966: The Stone-Mason's Funeral

*"Shaftsbury Stone Mason and Son Die Under Wheels of Vt. Rail-
way Train While Hunting"—Bennington (Vt.) Banner,* November 23, 1966

1

"Are you there, son?" "Here. All here."

I think of the wheels: what the wheels meant:

the cement-mixer by the walled garden,
its conical jet's nose
kneading quicklime, semen, cement,
tilted and turning . . .

and the half-naked ones
seen from above—the son, the father, the son—
filling the troughs of cement
at the great wall's center, in the stone-mason's way:
the stone rose, the stone heart of the artichoke,
the marrow and block of the burning—

or drinking cold cokes in the cavernous lilac,
the sun on their nipples, their nostrils, their sex,

on their backs, and at rest.

2

I think of the hunt: what the father was hunting,
paring boulders to bone,
angling and shunting the wedges
of granite, fitting facets like pineapple-rind, forcing rubble
and shell like flint for an arrowhead—

what was he hunting there, with the hod on his shoulders
and the brick and the straw of the Hebrews behind him,
the Great Wall of China, the tower, the well,
the winnowing wheels and the millstones of Gaza,
the tables of bran and macadam—

what would strike through the granite to find him?

3

I think of the wall: what the stones meant:
the son, the father, the son,
piling their burial barrow in the nightshade and lilac,
in the cold sweat of Adam:

what blackened the boulders with the horn
of the Scyldings,
circled the rooftops
of Stonehenge, the quarries of Syracuse,
the monoliths
pointing their profiles toward Easter Island
like the dial of a petrified garden:

what were they building
to make an unbreakable world in the dews of the terrace?

4

"Are you there, son?" "Here. All here."
                                    "Keep
your flashes down low. Feel for the brush with your toes,
drop onto your heels, and set them down light.
No use to startle the deer in the dark."

"Right."

"Watch for the horns of the buck. Stand clear
of the does. We'll double on back
where the path takes the turn by the overhang
and crosses the railroad track.

"Good luck."

5

I think of the wheels: what the wheels meant:

the barred box-cars, the freights passing over
a seamed span of track like a carpenter's
rule opened flat to its length
in the gravel and thistle—

cow-catcher, lanterns, and cistern, the rust of the trestle,
the switch—

then a spindle of light like a burning
glass focused on nothing, frosting the clover like glass,
the acidulous smell of the sand on the spikes and the steel
of the crossties—the whistle . . .

till the ruby that held the caboose to its track
spiraled into the jewel of a railroader's watch
and clicked shut—

and the journey was over.

6

I think of their deaths: what their deaths meant:

having set the last boulder
with the stone-mason's cunning that steadies the block
from within, in the pith
of cement, showing only the coarse outer edges, and the spaces
dividing the stones, held in precarious balance
like a zodiac circling a sun—

the son, the father, the son,
pursuing the deer
over crossties of mica like stepping-stones cut for the path
of the steam's effervescence, the whistle, the wheel, and the scream—

having come to the place they had sought: the underground
door in the green of the terraces,
the mastodon's mound in the nightshade and bittersweet:
having said:

> "We have seen antler and horn in the labyrinth."

they sealed the great threshold, set the altar-stone over the plinth,
signed the mortar and bricks
with a wreath of initials and three copper pennies

dated: *one nine six six.*

Moon Walk

It is time to re-invent life,
we say, smelling ammonia from Mars
in a photograph, seeing right angles
in galactic soda, a glass bead from a crater,
the color purple.

        To that enormous death's head
we bring the constellation of Snoopy and Charlie Brown
in a comic-strip balloon of antiphonal beeps,
with a virus's chemical courage, trailing a ration
of air in plexiglass and nylon, printing
a square of carbon like a tennis court,
planting our human shadow and contamination.

A hammer taps: *It is later than you think.*
                      We follow
the White Rabbit through the lunar asparagus,
gathering specimens for the radiologist, peer
into the pockets of Alice's pinafore, grown infinitesimal,
fall into the daydream of the hookah and the caterpillar
and the Sea of Tears.

Still something haunts us from that other life—
di Chirico's light, Dalí's pebble seen at six o'clock,
our radical loneliness, our bereavement, our
conspiratorial nostalgia for transcendence. We hear
volcanic tumblers turning in the rock, walk
toward the blinded mirror's other side, and:

                                    "Do not die!"
we say: "Old fire-eater, huntress, menstrual mother,
do not die! See—we bring you a feather
from that other life, an answering mirror to take
the living exhalation of your breath!"
                              And wait
by the death-bed for an acknowledging eye
to open, as Wordsworth's children did.
                          A "simple
Child that feels its life in every limb,"
(the poet said): "What should it know of death?"

IV

A Gift of Light

The Orphaning

1. *A Failed Rage*

Clear Idiot, I understand.
                              The adversary
need not be struck, or the blow
returned. Your foreknowledge of the deed
is enough, and proves mighty. You named it Innocency:
the receptive faculty, the negative power, and wore it
under the recoil of the loved hand and the hated hand,
falling equally, falling always. You said:
"Yes, I know. The blow comes as I knew it would come.
I foresaw it all. I am not angry." You turned
into your secrecy, smiled for a world's
perfidy, and denied yourself the act.

                    All this was false.

The act alone is innocent, and sweetens.
The child strikes with his fist in the womb's haven
and the father replies in the lover's spasm. Spend.
Reply. What was kept, has betrayed you. See:
the rage fails, the restorative rage, and the hate
talks with its cause over the infamous pit,
touching nothing.
              Your awkwardness with tools, all
the gear of action, your poor record at the shooting range,
are the fruit of a denial. Raise the gun to your shoulder.
It is heavier than you knew. Slam the bolt to.
It will not lock to your blow.

Only what is given, is. Only the act returns.
                            Be returned.

2. Ash-Mound

It is time you named your enemy.
Your instruments have devoured you: the poem,
the kiss, the loss, the image, the afterthought,
the orphan in the disinfected corridor
crying: *Integrity!* like Job on the ash-mound.
Your compass moved upon Self, always, as on a dial,
when you thought to pass beyond
it, magnetic to your incompletion. "Choice"
was a compass's fiction, and "control,"
only the needle's need to point to the Self
when Possibility opened beyond,
and tremble to a standstill there. Always
volition lay outside, deep in the play of the act
itself—free, bold, availing, neither enemy
nor friend, partial or entire, chosen or compelled.

3. *A Gift of Light*

Mother, in that darkness into which you go,
which is not Lear's or Homer's—not Charon's
bowsprit bearing the devious Florentine
on the downward eddy to allegorical heaven:
nothing dreamt or dissembled, or given the spirit to know,
to prove it precarious, like thirst or the gift of tears,
but blindness itself, a smashing of lenses and lives—
why does my childhood tremble, and my gaze go up
with a child's assurance, for the large, loved hand
of that providing walker who measures her stride to my own
and steadies the balances?
                For I guess at a thing
not desolation's, and walk, as toward birthdays, with
all my surprise made ready.

You come with a gift of light,
mulish and brave, in the shine of sabbatical
candles, wearing my blindness; not
in the barbiturate sleep of the maimed, but held in the salt
of a photograph, parting conventional hedges, a rich braid caught
on the serious smile and the Ukrainian stance,
by an apron of porches.
                              And all is returned in a dazzle, half
seen, like the eylash's arc on the eye when the sleeper wakens.
Poppyseed burns on my lips. We mount up the kiosk
together, my trust in your hand, like a forfeit,
climbing the steps of my nausea,
while the bell-tower tips toward the dial of the Orphanage
clock, and the iron opens outward. There, all my sullen deprival
surrenders its lonely disguises.
                              There is my father,
clear in the long halation; there, the ascending staves of the bed,
harplike in peeling enamel, where I listen to prodigies; there,
grave-plot, head-stone, prayer-shawl,
where the son of the blessing arises,
the sevenfold tape on his forearm, and remembers the prayer for the dead.
A stone in the grave of his mouth moves
and he cries from the grave-clout: *Father!*

and forgives him his dying, who knew not what he did.

4. *Wedding Dance*

In the Home For the Blind,
the ramps plunge under their double harness of rails
like a gymnast's parallels

or a ballerina's barre, to call the blind outdoors
and tilt them toward the gardens. There,
in the tinny brilliance and the braille

of grassy quadrants, my mother waits by the burnished iron
like a dancer by her glass, for the ticking cane,
the cuffs-links and the cloth of her blinded dancing partner

that draws her failing balance
toward his arm, opens a lane in soiled, suburban air,
and guides her broken footing through the dance.

The space is full of rings,
thresholds, spikes of flying nylon, dangerous metal,
falls on the netted causeways underneath the swings,

as my mother tries her toe-hold on the wire,
prehensile as a sea-bird, breaks out a blind
umbrella, and rides the blazing slant, into her *shtetl*.

She has her heart's desire
again—the moon and the fiddle, the night-skies
of Chagall, whirled on the thermal currents toward the rafters

in a bride-groom's *pas-de-deux*,
past Dante's second circle and Abraham's laughter:
"Shall Sara, that is ninety years old, bear?"

My mother holds the tightwire
like a plummet. Her partner, at his ease,
levels the pure progressions of his arc,

and tops the trees. His cuff-links glint in the sun. All
is impeccable: the star-turn of the happy aerialist,
flier and flier caught on a stilled trapeze,

till the air is suddenly darker, a wind blows
cold from the used graveyard where, out of my father's eyes,
I watch the dancers print the burnt grass and move into the shadows.

5. A Stone Raised

When you turned from us, in your coma,
and we fought on the terrible starch of your bed
to contain your wracked pulse-beat in our circle
of unspoken bereavement,
I heard a sound like the breaking of ash in a crater
where once, in the water-sheds
binding my breath to your breast,
knees to my chin,
I slept under your heart—

                        and I broke from the circle
and said:

            "Put me out of your mind; put on your death;
            rest. Grief cannot matter
            in the long degradation
            of blindness, maimed memory lost
            to itself, the great
            faultings of love by which the living interpret
            trespass and probity—all that forces your spirit
            to sweat in the flint and the trash of the earth like a slave
            to win us survival. Take
            up your bed and your grave
            and walk forth to your peace."

Now I would reckon
the whole cost of our greed,
who would have the dead with us—
alive to us only in the indecent duress of their breathing—
because they still work in our pulses.
How much better that the lost and unseeing
should see through our need, in the end, foretell
our heart's changes, pass on to non-being,
knowing all would be well with us?

All is well with me, Mother.
Holding the great shell of your heart
in my hands, I hear the whole power of its passion
move through my fears, with its buoys and its bells
in a tilting horizon of undertow:

your blood and your milk still encompass me;
you walk through the gums and the leaves of midsummer,
first at the gates of my Sunday, with a paper
cornucopia under each hand:

There is nothing to own or disown,
nothing left to commemorate,
as now, in the year of your wish,
filling the sky like a birth-mark or a ripened placenta,
knowing the rite to be good,
I bend toward your death with this stone.

V

In Two Voices

Little Testament

(Piccolo Testamento)

This thing that darkles and dazzles at night
in the husk of my head—
snailtrack in mother-of-pearl,
smashed emery glass—it could never
light up a church or a work-table
or be trimmed like a lamp by the black and the red
of the clerical.
Eye's apple, iris: it is all
I can give as my warranty:
Faith's keepsake, an embattled presumption that burned
like a hard log on a hearth, at long length.
Look well to the ashes, in that mirror
when all the lamps gutter
and the pace of the dancer is timed to a hellish
sardana, and Lucifer, Prince of Darkness, is seen
on a bowsprit on the Thames or the Seine or the Hudson,
beating bituminous wings, half
shorn from his shoulders with the strain of it. "Time's up!"
he will tell you. This thing that I leave is no charm
against hurricane
hung on a cobweb of memory:
but histories end and begin in a cinder
and only extinction is viable.
The sign was a lucky one: whoever has seen it
cannot fail to retrieve you.

Like calls to like: our pride was no trick
of escape, nor our meekness
ignoble, and the tenuous glimmer
that we grated down there was not struck by the stick of a match.

(Eugenio Montale)

The Balcony

(Il Balcone)

The gambit seemed easy—
a change to annihilate space
where it opened for me: the blaze
of your certainty turned into quizzical tedium.

Now I contract, in that void,
all my tardy volition:
out of bitter non-being, there flashes
the will to attend you, alive.

That life, shedding lustre—
you acknowledged no other—
you lean to it now from that window
which never grows lighter.

(Eugenio Montale)

Abel Martín: Last Lamentations

(Últimas Lamentaciones de Abel Martín)

This spring day, I dreamed
that a delicate body, my amenable
double in shadow, moved with me. The body
of boyhood it seemed,
leaping the treads of a stairway, three at a bound.
—you, there! You, yesterday's greyhound!
(A light like a lighted aquarium,
seachange of mirrors that deepened
its rancid effulgence in a carrion corner of ashes.)
—Still with me, young playfellow?
                              —Still with you, old father!

And dreamed then the gallery
and the garden of cypress and lemons:
a languishing pigeon warming the cold of a stone,
red kites over indigo blues;
and that ward of my childhood, austerest angel of all,
keeping watch on a magical anguish.

Absence and distance,
the tunics of morning: I could tell
them again in my dream—poised taut on a bow-line's resistance,
day's arrow, the vision that ends in a scream:
the burst of the flame in the fuse
and the charge in the shell . . .

(Antonio Machado)

Greatness Abounding

(Al Gran Pleno)

Let him ponder that sovereign Zero—statued
in bleakest marble
and frowning austerely,
one hand supporting its cheek—
by the wide backwaters of the river,
time without end, by the water's margin;
peace to his rest who slumbers forever and ever.
And that divinest logic
which imagines,
the undissembling image—
(enough of mirrors! the fountain-burst is all!)—
say it: let be whatever exists, let whatever
discloses itself be seen. Serene and strenuous
—the sea and the fish and the living hook for the fish,
the whole of the sea in a droplet, all
fish in the single egg,
and all of it new—let each
make its separate sign and be unanimous.
All keeps its appointed place, all moves
and reflects
and is changed like a changing coin as it goes:
a dream moving this way and that. Love
keeps the nettle, the rose:
the kernel of wheat and the poppy
bring it forth in a single seed.
That harmony! All sings

in the day's meridian:
effaces the faces of Zero,
turns to its vision, seeing
where the bubble boils in the spring,
the vehement waters of being.

(*Antonio Machado*)

La Recoleta

Death is scrupulous here; here, in this city of ports,
death is circumspect:
a blood-kinship of enduring and provident light
reaching out from the courts of the *Socorro,*
from the ash burnt to bits in the braziers,
to the sugar-and-milk of a holiday treat
and a depth of patios like a dynasty.
Old sweetnesses, old rigors meet
and are one in the graveyards of *La Recoleta.*

At your summit, the portico's bravery,
a tree's blind solicitude,
birds prattling of death without ever suspecting it,
a ruffle of drums from the veteran's burial plot
to hearten the bypasser;
at your shoulder, hidden away, the tenements of the North-side,
the walls of the executioner, Rosas.
Here a nation of unrepresentable dead
thrives on decay under a suffrage of marble,
since the day that the earliest seed in your garden, destined for heaven,
Uruguay's child,
María de los Dolores Maciel, dropped off to sleep—
the least of your buried—in your waste desolation.

Here something holds me: I think
of the fatuous flowers that speak out so piously now in your name—
the leaf-yellow clay under the fringe of acacia,
memorial wreaths lifted up in your family crypts—
why do they stay here, in their sleepy and delicate way,
side by side with the terrible keepsakes of those whom we loved?

I put the hard question and venture an answer:
our flowers keep perpetual watch on the dead
because we all incomprehensibly know
that their sleepy and delicate presence
is all we can offer the dead to take with them in their dying,
without giving offense through the pride of our living
or seeming more alive than the dead.

(*Jorge Luis Borges*)

We Eat Shadow

(Comemos Sombra)

The whole of you, unknowable power that never discloses itself.
Power that we sometimes invite with the thrust of our loving.
There, we come on a knot. We finger a body,
a spirit, we encircle it so, and we say: "Now I have you!" Morosely,
complacently, at leisure, we explore all the trials of the chance for whose sake we
      were warned.
Here is the head, here the breast, here the profile and flight,
the swift inundation, the escape, the ripe legs in their sweetness, that appear to
      flow out and stand still eternally.
And we narrow our living tumescence a moment.
We acknowledge the truth in our arms, the desirable body, the overheard spirit,
the spirit so avidly coveted.

But where does it come from—love's power, the similitude given us here with a
      God's reciprocity,
a God who begrudges us nothing, sets no limit on loving, plucks us out, spirit
      and body, to solace us here in his name?
We stand with the crumb in our mouths and are quiet, like dogs, we go on,
we encarnate ourselves in the obdurate splendor, intent on our hunger,
we strain toward whatever is flung to us here by a hand.
But where does it come from, the singular hand that would offer
its great gifts of suavity, your infinite skin,
your singular truth, the caress that can quiet our breathing and stays on, without
      end?

Half-dead, we look up. Table-scraps,
bread-crusts, the whip-lash, our rage, our living and dying:
you scatter them out to all sides, as if you would deal us your pity,
you fling us a shadow, while a glitter glows under our teeth,
an echo's resplendance, an echo's re-echo re-echoed: a splendor;
and we eat what is given.
We eat shadow, we gorge on the dream or the shadow, and are quiet.
We are struck with an awe: and we sing. Love is your name.

But later, the eyes, humid and huge, lift up. The hand
is no more. Not so much as a rustle
of cloth can be heard.
Only a great sound of weeping, or the silence's tension.
The silence that is all we can take with us
when, in the teeth of the vanishing shadow, now grown ravenous, we launch
ourselves onward again.

(Vicente Aleixandre)